CONTENTS

IMPRESSIONS OF NEW YORK

I. Strolling the Upper West Side

By MONA REJINO

IMPRESSIONS OF NEW YORK

FOR VIOLA (OR VIOLIN), CELLO, AND PIANO

BY MONA REJINO

ISBN: 978-1-5400-4661-1

Contact us:
Hal Leonard
7777 West Bluemound Road
Milwaukee, WI 53213
Email: info@halleonard.com

In Europe, contact:
Hal Leonard Europe Limited
42 Wigmore Street
Marylebone, London, W1U 2RN
Email: info@halleonardeurope.com

In Australia, contact:
Hal Leonard Australia Pty. Ltd.
4 Lentara Court
Cheltenham, Victoria, 3192 Australia
Email: info@halleonard.com.au

FROM THE COMPOSER

I have always loved collaborating with other musicians, whether on duets, ensembles, or chamber works. I was thrilled and honored to receive an invitation to compose a trio for the MTNA Composer Commissioning Program to be premiered at the 2019 Conference. The proposed instrumentation of viola, cello, and piano was a perfect fit since my daughter is a violist, my son is a cellist, and I am a pianist. I included an optional violin part in place of the viola to make the trio accessible to more student performers.

Creating interesting melodies, rich harmonies, and adding a touch of jazz has been my goal in writing this composition. *Impressions of New York* explores the sights and sounds one might encounter when visiting this vibrant city. The first movement, *Strolling the Upper West Side*, has a suave, sophisticated feel. You can imagine walking down a tree-lined street in this lovely neighborhood on a beautiful, sunny day. The second movement, *Midnight in Brooklyn*, exudes a slow, sultry mood. Picture yourself sitting in a club late at night as the day winds down, being transformed by the music of a fine jazz trio. The final movement, *Grand Central Station*, has a frenetic pace depicting scores of people rushing through this crowded architectural giant, as they race from one train to another to reach their destination. The third movement is the most technical of all. Rhythmically, the beat shifts from a feeling of 6/8 to 3/4 throughout, almost leaving you breathless as it drives to the finish.

I am indebted to Dr. Ann Rivers Witherspoon for her leadership on this project, the fine musicians at the University of Missouri for their expertise, my colleagues at the Hockaday School for their invaluable suggestions, and Don Dillon for his generous engraving. My hope is that this trio will provide a rewarding musical experience for those who perform it, as well as for those who hear it performed.

–Mona Rejino

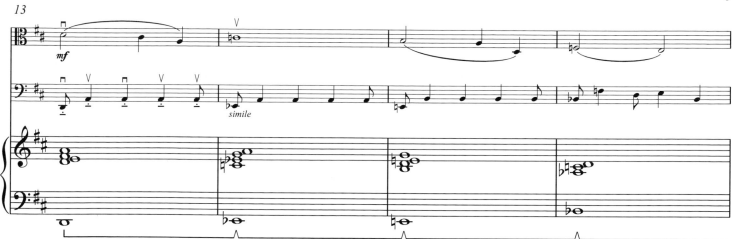

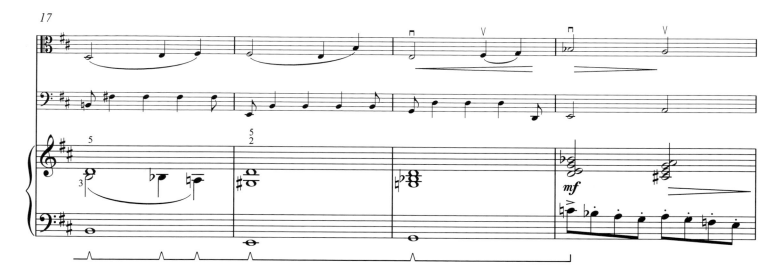

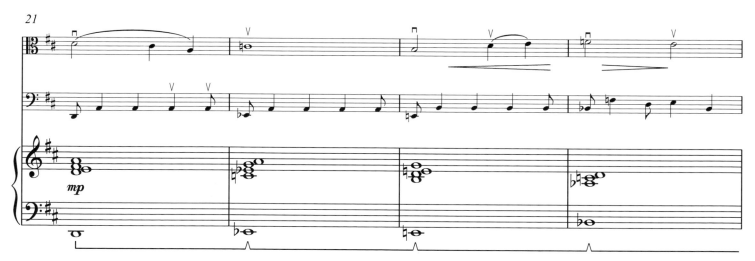

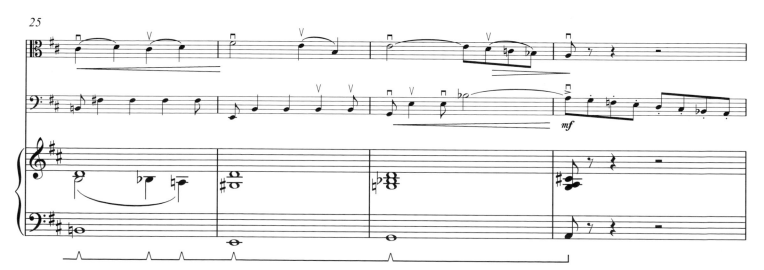

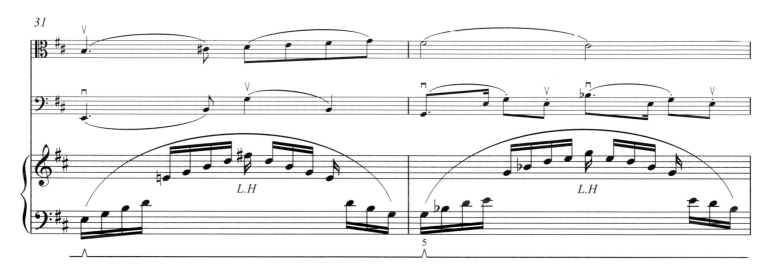

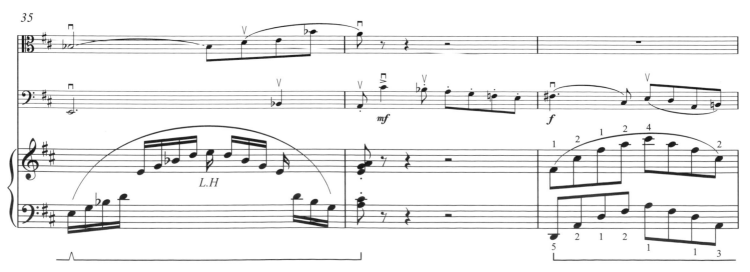

II. Midnight in Brooklyn

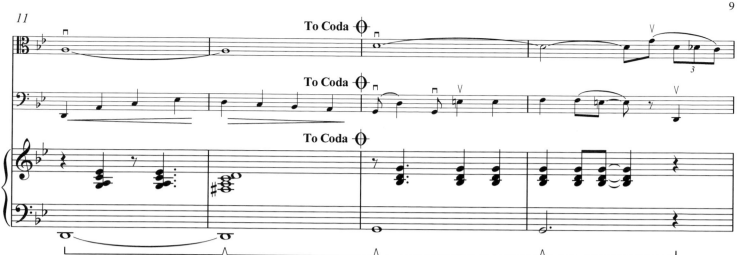

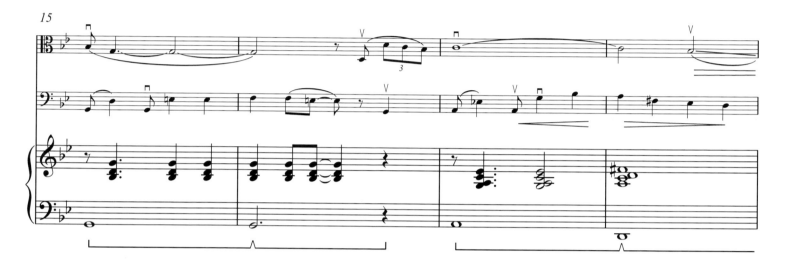

III. Grand Central Station

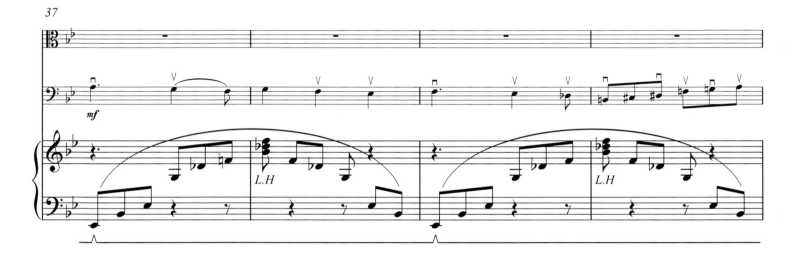

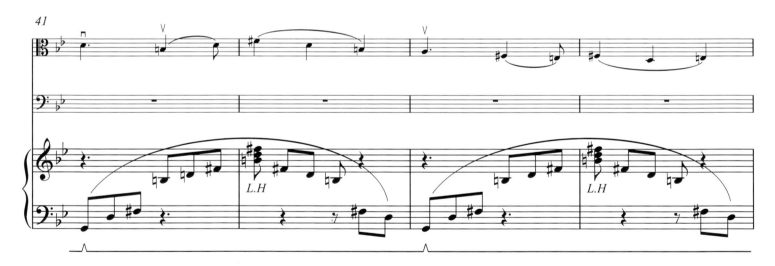

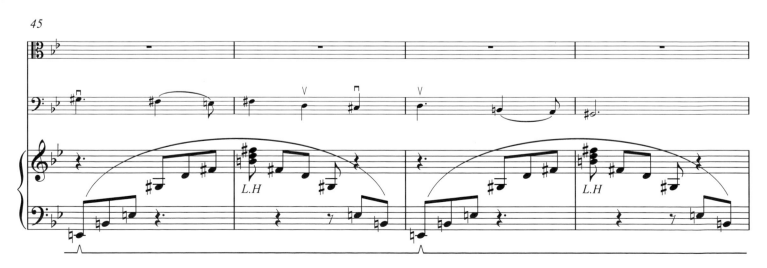

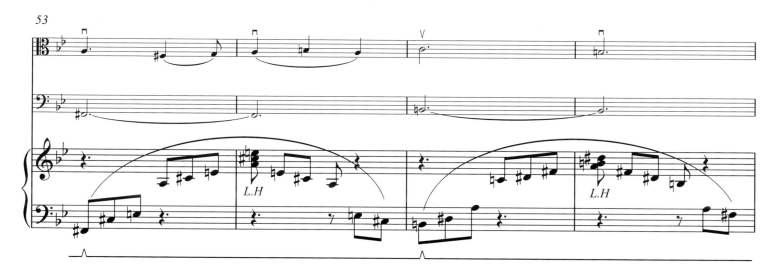

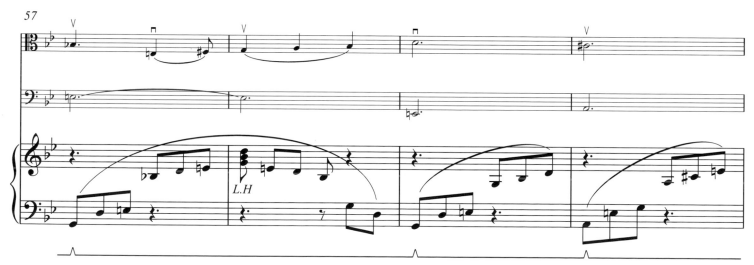

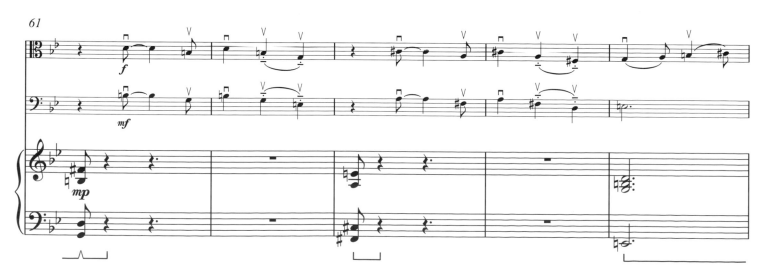

IMPRESSIONS OF NEW YORK
I. Strolling the Upper West Side

Viola

By MONA REJINO

II. Midnight in Brooklyn

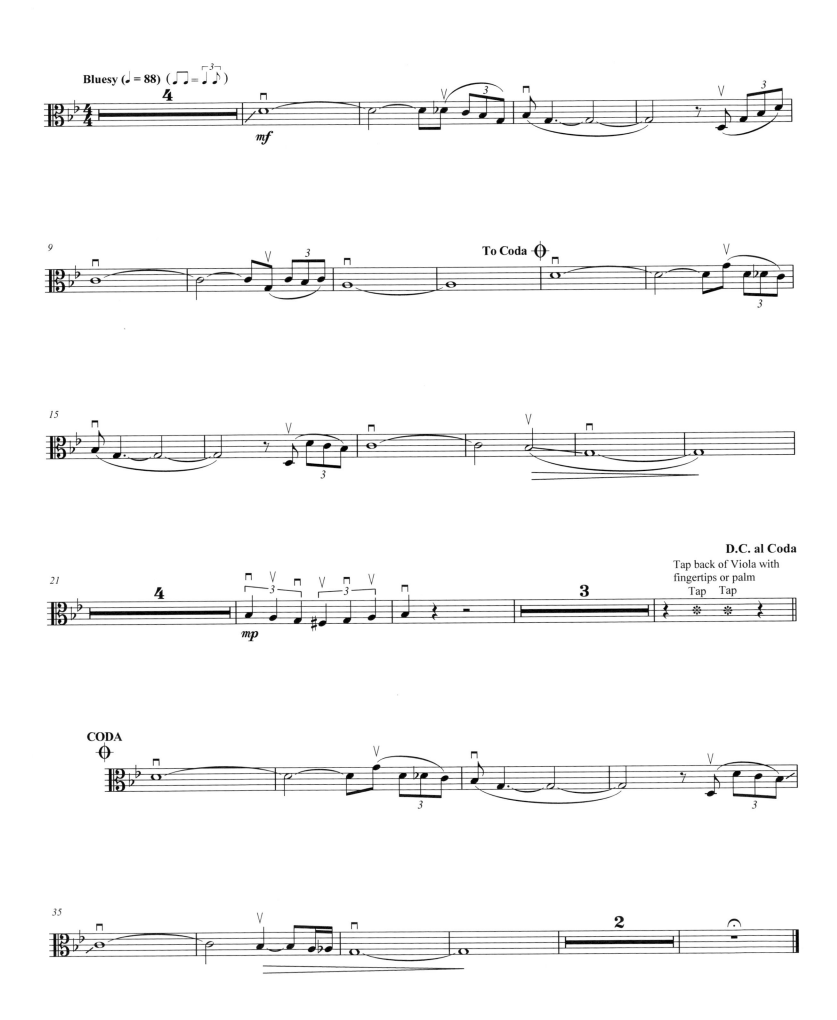

III. Grand Central Station

IMPRESSIONS OF NEW YORK
I. Strolling the Upper West Side

Violoncello

By MONA REJINO

II. Midnight in Brooklyn

III. Grand Central Station

IMPRESSIONS OF NEW YORK
I. Strolling the Upper West Side

By MONA REJINO

Violin
(Optional in place of Viola)

II. Midnight in Brooklyn

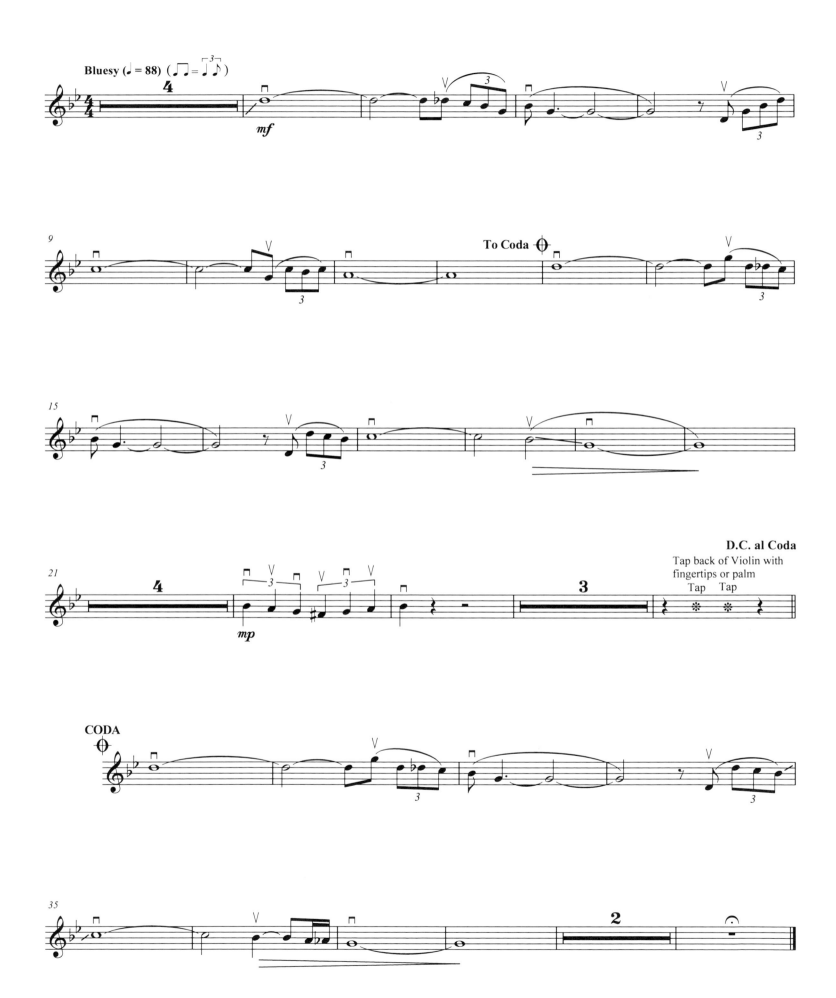

III. Grand Central Station